ANCIENT
SCOTLAND

ANCIENT SCOTLAND

Iain Zaczek

PHOTOGRAPHY BY
David Lyons

First published in Great Britain in 1998 by
Collins & Brown Limited
London House, Great Eastern Wharf,
Parkgate Road, London SW11 4NQ

British Library Cataloguing-in-Publication Data:
A catalogue record for this title is available
from the British Library.

1 3 5 7 9 8 6 4 2
ISBN 1 85585 496 1 (hardback edition)
ISBN 1 85585 646 8 (paperback edition)

Conceived, edited and designed by
Collins & Brown Limited

Editorial Director Sarah Hoggett
Art Director Roger Bristow
Editors Katie Bent and Mandy Greenfield
Designer Bill Mason

Map on p. 6 by Andrew Farmer

Printed and bound in Hong Kong

FRONT COVER: North Uist, Pobull Fhinn stone circle
on Ben Langass

BACK COVER: Cross-slab, Aberlemno, Angus

HALF TITLE: Caerlaverock Castle, Dumfries

FRONTISPIECE: Mull, Strathclyde, across Loch Na Keal
towards the slopes of Ben More

ACKNOWLEDGEMENTS

David Lyons – My thanks to Keith Bowden of Historic Scotland and
all the people on the ground who pointed me in the right direction,
fortified with a cup of tea or a dram.

In particular I am indebted to Rachel Butter and David Clough
at the Kilmartin House Centre for Archaeology and Landscape
Interpretation, for their inspiring hospitality and for providing a
most stimulating venue for the discussion of Ancient Scotland. 'Lang
may their chimney reek.'

Iain Zaczek – I am grateful for the advice and support I have received
from many friends and colleagues. In particular, I would like to
express my thanks to Ian Chilvers, Caroline Bugler, Ann Farquhar,
Ernst Haverkamp, Caroline Juler, Lesley Lonie, Ross and Margaret
Millar, John Norris and Helen Mowat. Thanks also to Mandy
Greenfield for her very helpful additions to the text.

CONTENTS

MAP OF ANCIENT SCOTLAND

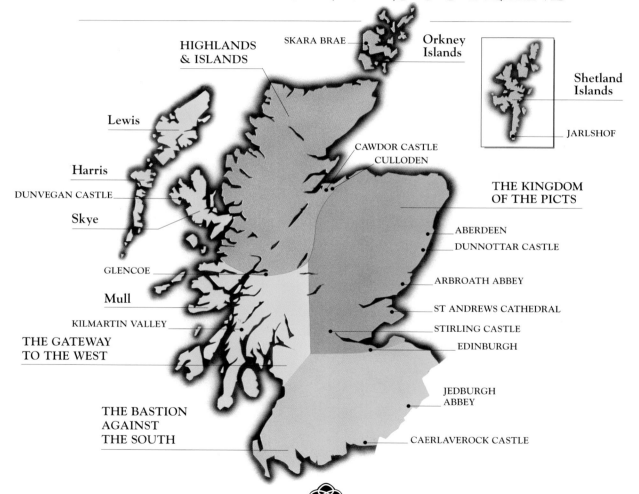

HIGHLANDS & ISLANDS

SKARA BRAE

Orkney Islands

Shetland Islands

JARLSHOF

Lewis

Harris

DUNVEGAN CASTLE

Skye

CAWDOR CASTLE
CULLODEN

THE KINGDOM OF THE PICTS

ABERDEEN

DUNNOTTAR CASTLE

GLENCOE

Mull

ARBROATH ABBEY

ST ANDREWS CATHEDRAL

KILMARTIN VALLEY

STIRLING CASTLE

EDINBURGH

THE GATEWAY TO THE WEST

JEDBURGH ABBEY

THE BASTION AGAINST THE SOUTH

CAERLAVEROCK CASTLE

INTRODUCTION

THE TRADITIONAL IMAGE OF the Scots is of a proud and fiercely independent people; rugged and fearless in times of war; loyal and resolute in times of peace. These qualities may well have been shaped by events, for the early inhabitants of Scotland had to battle constantly for survival. Their march towards nationhood was slow and arduous, hampered by the ongoing threat of domination by powerful neighbours or ruthless invaders.

The earliest struggles were against the elements themselves, for the prehistoric landscape was far from hospitable. The Ice Age lingered longer in Scotland than in many other parts of Europe and, as recently as 10,000 years ago, some areas were still affected. Even when the ice retreated, the terrain must have seemed a daunting prospect to early settlers. The range of mountains that bisected the country, running north-east to south-west, presented a formidable barrier. Elsewhere, much of the land was covered in dense tracts of wildwood or thick bogs. Not surprisingly, therefore, many of the initial inhabitants preferred to dwell along the coast or on offshore islands.

Some hints of living conditions during the neolithic era (c. 4000–2000 BC) can be gained from archaeological sites in the far north, at places like Skara Brae (see p. 23) and Knap of Howar (see p. 22). Fragments of fish and animal bones in the midden-heaps give a clear indication of diet, proving that these early people must have used boats for fishing out at sea. They may even have kept alive some small fish and crustaceans inside their houses, in special clay-lined, stone boxes, which have been interpreted as larder-pools. Other clues can be gleaned from the rich array of prehistoric tombs. The older ones took the form of large chambers, which were used for communal burials. These were invariably covered over with cairns, although access to the entrance was frequently left open, so that the chambers could be re-used. In time, these communal tombs gave way to single graves, often in stone cists. These were sometimes placed in the ritual circles – henges and recumbent stone circles – that had been erected by previous generations.

The emergence of identifiable tribes on the Scottish mainland is still a matter of controversy, although it is widely accepted that the ancestors of the Britons and the Picts established their first settlements during the Iron Age. With the arrival of the Roman legions, the picture becomes far clearer. Tacitus (c. AD 55–120) and other classical commentators put names to around a dozen tribes and these appeared on Ptolemy's map of the area, which dates from the 2nd century AD.

The Roman presence in Scotland spanned more than 300 years, beginning with Agricola's invasion of AD 79 and ending in 410. The results were mixed. On several occasions, it seemed as if total victory lay within Rome's grasp, but the decisive breakthrough always proved elusive. Agricola achieved a notable triumph at the battle of Mons Graupius (AD 84), but was recalled to Rome before he could consolidate it. The next expedition was undertaken by Antoninus Pius, who began his

LEFT: DUNADD FORT, ARGYLL

This rocky mount was the site of the first capital of Dalriada. It had the dual advantage of being close to the sea and easy to defend. Some ancient carvings have survived, among them the figure of a boar.

LEFT: MAES HOWE, ORKNEY

Vikings broke into this remarkable neolithic chambered cairn, constructed in c. 2700 BC, on several occasions, looting the grave-goods but leaving behind a series of carvings and Runic inscriptions.

northern push in AD 139 and tried to cement his gains by building the great, defensive wall that still bears his name. In this, he was disappointed. The Antonine Wall was completed by AD 144 and manned by around 6,000 soldiers. Even so, it was rapidly breached and many of the forts seem to have been abandoned following his death in 161.

During the period of occupation, the Romans were often on good terms with the Border tribes. Relations with the Votadini tribe, for example, appear to have been particularly close. This has been confirmed by the discovery of a hoard of Roman silver at their chief stronghold, Traprain Law in East Lothian.

Greater attention has been focused on the enemy tribes to the north. In the earliest Roman reports, the chief menace came from the Caledonians, but in 297 a writer named Eumenius spoke of a new group of raiders, sallying forth beyond Hadrian's Wall. These were the Picts ('the Painted Ones'), a fierce northern tribe who painted or tattooed their skin with strange designs. Throughout the 4th century they figured increasingly in the accounts of disturbances on the British frontier culminating in the onslaught of 367, when an alliance of different tribes attacked the Romans on all sides. The Picts streamed down from the north; the Scots and the Attacotti came from the west; while the Saxons attacked from the east.

The Scots, at this stage, were still living in Ireland, based in the small kingdom of Dalriada on the Ulster coast. They were a sea-faring race, and early reports describe them as pirates. This situation changed in *c.* 500 when, finding themselves threatened by other tribes in their traditional homeland, a party of Scots migrated to Argyll and founded a new colony of Dalriada.

The missionaries, who spread the Gospel in Scotland, also owed a debt to Ireland. The early achievements of the British-born St Ninian (*fl.* 390–400), were rapidly overshadowed by those of St Columba (*c.* 521–97), who arrived in Iona in 563. He introduced the ideas and organization of the Celtic Church, which did not conform precisely with those of the Papacy. The differences were eventually ironed out at the Synod of Whitby (664), when the Roman system was finally adopted. Even so, Celtic practices remained deep-rooted in Scotland.

Following the withdrawal of the Roman army, the Scottish mainland was beset by new enemies. Initially the most dangerous of these appeared to be the Angles, a Germanic tribe that gained a foothold in Britain in the 5th century. In 605 they

LEFT: KEILLS CHAPEL, ARGYLL

The high crosses of Argyll and the Western Isles feature a blend of abstract Celtic patterns and stylized figures.

RIGHT: CRAIGNISH CHAPEL, ARGYLL

This 13th-century ruin stands on an early Christian site, dedicated to St Maelrubba of Applecross. It currently houses a fine collection of West Highland grave-slabs and four medieval tomb chests.

formed the powerful kingdom of Northumbria, after which they pressed on into Scotland. The Border kingdoms soon fell, the Scots suffered crushing defeats and it seemed as though the Picts, in their turn, might also be overrun. Eventually, though, the Angles were outwitted at the battle of Nechtansmere (685). Using a feigned retreat, the Picts managed to lure them into a

BELOW: DUNNOTTAR CASTLE, KINCARDINE

Besieged many times, Dunnottar's finest hour came during the Civil War, when it guarded the Scottish crown and sceptre.

narrow mountain pass, where they slaughtered them. The Lothians were not fully released from their grip until 1018, when Malcolm II gained a decisive victory at the battle of Carham. By this stage the Angles had made at least one lasting contribution to local culture: their language – English – had become the dominant form of speech in the region.

Once the threat of invasion had been removed, the Picts were able to resume their traditional rivalry with the Scots. Then, in the 790s, these feuds were interrupted by the emergence of a new breed of predator – the Vikings. In 795 they launched their first attack on Iona and, within a few years, the annals of other monasteries began to complain of similar attacks by a people whom they described as the 'foreigners', or the lochlann ('men of the lakes').

The Vikings (mainly Norwegians, in this instance) used the local terrain to good effect. Scotland has 787 islands around its coastline, an impossible number for the smaller kingdoms to defend. These provided temporary shelter and, as time went on, more permanent bases for the Viking longships. From an early stage, it is clear that the Orkneys and Shetlands served as winter havens for the raiding parties. At Jarlshof (see p. 21), for example, there were several workshops for repairing boats.

The Norsemen controlled the Western and Northern Isles for several hundred years, leaving an indelible mark on Scottish

RIGHT: EDINBURGH CASTLE, MIDLOTHIAN

Castle Rock has been occupied since the Bronze Age. The city's ancient name meant 'the fortress on the slope'.

culture. A host of place-names reflect Scandinavian roots, among them Cape Wrath (the 'turning point'), Pentland Firth ('Pictland Firth') and Sutherland (the 'land to the south'). The latter, which is actually the northernmost region of the Scottish mainland, illustrates perfectly the shifting balance of power, for many of the Earls of Orkney held Caithness, Sutherland and the Hebrides, along with the Northern Isles.

Ironically, the very strength of the Vikings helped to speed up the union of the Scots and the Picts. A series of attacks on Argyll and the west drove the Scots out of Dalriada, pushing them eastwards into Pictish territory. Then, in *c.* 843, the Scottish leader, Kenneth MacAlpin, secured the throne of his rivals, claiming Pictish descent through his mother's line. This presented him with the nucleus of the future Scottish nation.

MacAlpin and his immediate successors held much of the land north of the Forth, but it took time to regain the Scottish islands from their Norwegian overlords. The first real inroads were made by a man who was himself part Norse: Somerled ('the Summer Traveller'). In *c.* 1130 he raised a rebellion in the west, driving the Norsemen out of mainland Argyll. In 1156, with a powerful fleet of warships, he won a notable victory off the coast of Islay, giving him control of the southern Hebrides.

Somerled's successes were emulated by a number of Scottish kings. In 1196 William the Lion (1143–1214) seized northern Scotland from the Earls of Orkney, while Alexander III's defeat of King Haakon at Largs (1263) proved even more profitable. For, three years later, the remainder of the Hebrides was formally surrendered to him by the Treaty of Perth. The final

piece of the jigsaw was slotted into place in 1469, when James III (1451–88) married the daughter of the King of Norway and was granted the Orkneys and Shetlands as part of her dowry.

Long before this, Scotland's real concern had shifted towards her southern border. Following the Norman Conquest, the influence of the Anglo-Normans began to pose a growing threat, particularly during the reigns of Malcolm Canmore (ruled 1058–93) and David I (ruled 1124–53), both of whom had been raised in England. They distributed wealth and favours to their Norman friends, arousing suspicions of an English take-over. In fact, this did not happen until the end of the 13th century, when Edward I took advantage of a succession crisis by launching an invasion. This met with stern resistance, led by the two famous outlaw-heroes, William Wallace (*c.* 1274–1305) and Robert the Bruce (1274–1329). They won rousing victories at Stirling Bridge (1297) and Bannockburn (1314). The patriotic fervour inspired by this struggle demonstrated that the country had at last assumed the mantle of nationhood. Nothing illustrates this more forcibly than the battle-cry in the Declaration of Arbroath (1320), Scotland's declaration of independence: 'We fight not for glory, nor riches, nor honour, but only for that liberty which no true man relinquishes but with his life.'

RIGHT: GLENCOE, ARGYLL

The beauty of Glencoe will always be tainted by the memory of the infamous massacre of 1692. Although it took place in a remote corner of Scotland, the scale of the treachery caused outrage countrywide.

HIGHLANDS
& ISLANDS

THE MOST SPECTACULAR reminders of Scotland's ancient past can be found in its northernmost region, whose very remoteness has helped preserve a rich array of prehistoric sites. The nature of the environment has also played an important part. In some areas the scarcity of timber, coupled with the ready availability of soft, red sandstone – which can be split easily into slabs, using the most basic tools – persuaded ancient builders to work almost exclusively in stone. At sites like Skara Brae (see p. 23), even objects such as beds, storage boxes and cupboards of stone have survived, providing archaeologists with a clear, physical image of everyday life in prehistoric times.

LEFT: LOCH INCHARD, SUTHERLAND

Noted for its wild birds and seals, the panoramic splendour of Loch Inchard is situated a few miles south of the windswept headland of Cape Wrath.

ABOVE: CLAVA CAIRNS, INVERNESS

The three cairns at Clava are neolithic chamber tombs, set within a stone circle. One is a ring cairn, while the other two have entrance passages.

The earliest settlers were farmers, who lived by fishing, rearing sheep and cultivating cereal crops, and the oldest surviving houses date from the 4th millennium BC. These farmers built a series of impressive communal graves, mostly taking the form of chambered cairns. The latter came in many shapes and sizes – long, circular, heel-shaped or divided into 'stalls'. The great henge monuments, such as the Ring of Brodgar (see pp. 24–5) and the Stones of Stenness (see pp. 26–7), are thought to date from the end of this period.

It seems that a cooling of the climate slowed developments during part of the Bronze Age, but some evidence of metal-working can be found. At Jarlshof (see p. 21) archaeologists recovered the stock of a bronze smith working in *c.* 650 BC.

The design of contemporary, domestic architecture suggests that everyday life was comparatively peaceable at this time, but a dramatic change was already under way. As the Iron Age progressed, buildings acquired a more fortified character. These ranged from the sturdy blockhouse at Clickhimin (see p. 20) to the towering brochs, which are so closely associated with the Northern Isles. The name 'broch' derives from the Norse word *borg* (meaning 'defence'), but the structures predated the Viking raids by many centuries. In essence, they were two-storeyed, circular buildings, which could rise to 10.6 metres (35 feet). Their heyday is traditionally assigned to the first two centuries AD, although there is increasing evidence that they originated much earlier, and some may have been occupied by successive generations for as long as a millennium.

The events that lay behind the creation of the brochs are tantalizingly unclear, but there are hints that inter-tribal warfare, piracy and slave-raiding were becoming a problem. Archaeologists have recovered some weapons, among them decorated slingshots and the bone handles of fire-spears (flaming brands of wood were attached to these handles).

Some of the northern warlords appear to have been fairly powerful. There is a long-standing tradition that Orcadian chieftains made a treaty with the Romans in AD 43, and the influence of the islanders seems to have survived into the

Pictish period. For it is recorded that Bridei (or Brude), son of Maelchon, a 6th-century Pictish king, demanded hostages from his vassals in the Orkneys, in order to keep them in check.

Although it lay outside their heartland, the Picts eventually came to dominate the far north. This is clear from the presence of a number of their characteristic symbol-stones. These include the trio of monuments on the Moray Firth coastline (see pp. 30–1) and the warrior scene at Birsay (see p. 28). The precise purpose of these stones is uncertain, although they are usually thought to mark territorial boundaries or the graves of local chieftains. Remains of Pictish buildings are less common: the best-preserved example is a house at Gurness, which has become known as 'the Shamrock', because the internal layout of its rooms resembles this leaf.

From the end of the 8th century, the Picts themselves came under threat from Viking raiders. Their attacks were mainly directed against the farmsteads, although there are hints that the search for booty was very thorough. A runic inscription in the prehistoric tomb of Maes Howe in the Orkneys (see p. 9) confirms that Viking intruders carried off 'a great treasure'.

Within a century, the Norsemen had formed permanent settlements in Caithness and the Northern Isles, establishing the Earldom of Orkney in c. 880. The first holder of the title was Sigurd Eysteinsson, who campaigned extensively in Sutherland, although his fame was eventually eclipsed by that of the 11th-century ruler, Thorfinn Sigurdsson, whose exploits on the Scottish mainland led him to become an ally of Macbeth. His grandson, Magnus, was later canonized, and the Orcadian cathedral at Kirkwall is dedicated to him. By this stage, Viking influence in the Highlands was waning, although the Northern Isles remained under Scandinavian control until the mid-15th century.

LEFT: GLENCOE, ARGYLL

The Glencoe massacre stemmed from William III's unpopularity in the Highlands. The MacDonalds had been slow to pledge allegiance to him, so William pressed the Campbells to help him take revenge.

CLICKHIMIN, LERWICK, SHETLAND

Above: THIS IMPORTANT SITE was occupied at several different periods, beginning in the late Bronze Age (*c.* 700–500 BC), when a simple farmstead was established. This was succeeded by a 'blockhouse' – a type of stone fort – and then by the huge, circular broch that still survives. During its heyday, around 60 people would have lived at the Clickhimin settlement. In the 2nd or 3rd century AD a wheelhouse was added to the complex.

JARLSHOF, SHETLAND

Right: JARLSHOF'S NORSE-SOUNDING name was invented by Sir Walter Scott, who visited the site in 1814 and used it as the setting for his novel, *The Pirate* (1821). Subsequent research has, however, revealed that some remains are significantly older, dating back to the 2nd millennium BC. Here, the foundations of a prehistoric house can be seen, together with a stone hearth and quern (a surface that was used for grinding corn).

KNAP OF HOWAR, ORKNEY

Left: THE KNAP OF HOWAR ('knoll of mounds') is the site of Orkney's oldest-known buildings. Its two neolithic houses, linked by a narrow passage, are thought to date from *c.* 3500 BC. Among the many finds at this site were fragments of pottery and flint tools, mallets made of antler and whalebone, and a polished stone axe.

SKARA BRAE, ORKNEY

Right: THIS EXTRAORDINARY neolithic village lay buried under sand for centuries, until a freak storm revealed its existence to archaeologists in 1850. Ten houses have survived, the oldest of which dates back to *c.* 3200 BC. Inside, the stone fittings provide a telling insight into the inhabitants' way of life. Here, a dresser and hearth can be seen, along with stone beds and larder-pools for fish.

RING OF BRODGAR, ORKNEY

Right: THE RING OF BRODGAR is both the most northerly and the most famous of Scotland's henges. In its original state, it formed a circle of 60 stones – 27 of which remain – with a diameter of 109 metres (120 yards). The site is probably related to the Stones of Stenness (see p. 26), which are situated just 1.6 km (1 mile) away.

Early visitors believed that these henges were sun temples, but recent research suggests that they may have been designed as lunar observatories. Whatever their purpose, they continued to fascinate later generations, for one of the stones bears a runic inscription.

STONES OF STENNESS, ORKNEY

Left and right: THE IMPOSING MONOLITHS at Stenness were once part of a henge, a ritual monument consisting of a stone circle and surrounding earthworks. Only four of the stones are still standing, but originally there were 12. Radiocarbon tests on animal and charcoal deposits found at the site indicate that the henge dates back to the 3rd millennium BC. In more recent times, it was the centre of a popular fertility cult. Local couples would make their vows within the circle and then join hands at the nearby Stone of Odin – a single standing stone, which was destroyed in 1814.

BROUGH OF BIRSAY, ORKNEY

Above: BIRSAY IS A TIDAL ISLAND, occupying an important, strategic position at the north-western tip of Orkney's mainland. The Picts settled here, erecting one of their most elaborate symbol-stones, decorated with three large warriors. Under the Vikings, Birsay became the seat of the Earls of Orkney, most notably Thorfinn Sigurdsson, who built a church on the site.

BROCH OF GURNESS, ORKNEY

Right: THE SETTLEMENT AT Gurness spans many centuries, beginning in the Iron Age, when the massive broch was constructed. Among later inhabitants were the Picts and Vikings. The former left behind one of their earliest symbol-stones, dating from the 6th century, while the principal Viking find was the tomb of a woman, laid to rest with bronze jewellery and iron implements.

PICTISH STONES, SHANDWICK

THE MONUMENT AT SHANDWICK is one of three ancient crosses that were erected along a short stretch of the Moray Firth coastline. These crosses – at Nigg, Hilton of Cadboll, and Shandwick itself – are said to mark the burial spots of shipwrecked Viking princes. The spiral pattern (below), featured on one of the stone panels, is typical of Celtic design throughout Europe, but the hunting scene (left) is more characteristic of Pictish art. Here, riders and archers mingle with a decorative array of stags, hounds and outlandish birds.

Durness, Sutherland

Right: DURNESS IS A WILD and lonely spot, not far from Cape Wrath, the north-western tip of Scotland. Today sheep-farming is the staple industry, but the area has known its share of darker trades. The most notorious local inhabitant was Donald MacMurchov (d. 1619), a highwayman who tried to atone for his crimes by endowing Durness Old Church. Legend also tells of Donald, the Wizard Laird of Reay, who confronted the Devil in nearby Smoo Cave. The laird managed to escape, although he lost his shadow in the process.

GREY CAIRNS OF CAMSTER

Above: THE PREHISTORIC COMPLEX at Camster consists of three well-preserved chamber tombs. The example shown here is a long cairn, which measures 61 metres (200 feet) by 19.8 metres (65 feet) and has four projecting 'horns'. Close by there is also an impressive round cairn. Cremated remains and neolithic artefacts have been found on the site, most notably a fine, polished knife.

ARDVRECK CASTLE, SUTHERLAND

Right: NESTLING AT THE foot of Mount Quinag, the sparse ruins of Ardvreck Castle guard a treacherous secret. Here, the Marquess of Montrose, champion of the Scottish Royalists, was arrested and sent to Edinburgh for execution in the High Street on 21 May 1650. Some believe he was betrayed by Macleod of Assynt, who sold him to the Cromwellians for a £25,000 reward, but this is hotly disputed.

RANNOCH MOOR, PERTHSHIRE

Above: THIS PEATY WASTELAND WAS ONCE part of the great Caledonian Forest. Later, the wildness of the place made it an ideal refuge for brigands and outlaws. Sir William Wallace and Robert the Bruce both sheltered here during their struggles against the English, while superstitious folk believed that it was a haunt of the kelpie, a malevolent water-sprite that appeared in the shape of a ghostly horse.

GLENCOE, ARGYLL

Above: THE NAME OF GLENCOE (literally the 'glen of weeping') will always be linked with one of the most shameful episodes in Scottish history. During the night of 13 February 1692, as a blanket of snow carpeted the valley, members of the Campbell clan went from cottage to cottage, slaughtering their rivals, the MacDonalds. The massacre was viewed with particular horror, as the Campbells had been staying as guests of their victims.

Castle Tioram, Inverness

Right: Castle Tioram, or Tirrim, stands on a rocky promontory at the edge of Loch Moidart. When the waters are high, this becomes an island. Much of the castle dates back to the early 13th century, though the high tower was added in *c.* 1600. For centuries it was the principal stronghold of the MacDonalds of Clanranald. They were firm supporters of the Jacobite cause, and in 1715, as members of the clan were leaving to join the uprising, the chief gave orders for the castle to be burned, to prevent it falling into Campbell hands.

LOCH LEVEN, ARGYLL

Left: THE SHORES OF LOCH LEVEN will always evoke memories of the massacre at Glencoe, seen here to the right, but they are also associated with a second atrocity. In 1752 James Stewart of Appin was unjustly hanged for the murder of Colin Campbell, a despised Crown official. Robert Louis Stevenson used this scandal as the basis for his novels, *Kidnapped* (1886) and *Catriona* (1893).

ROGIE FALLS, ROSS & CROMARTY

Below: NOW A PEACEFUL BEAUTY spot, where picnickers relax by watching the salmon leap, this district was once the scene of violent conflicts. At Knockfarrel there is a vitrified fort, perhaps erected by the Picts, while at Kinellan there was a fierce battle between the MacDonalds and the MacKenzies. This resulted in the former losing their title of Lords of the Isles.

LOCH GARRY, INVERNESS

Left: THIS REGION WAS TRADITIONALLY held by the MacDonalds of Glengarry. Their family seat was at the nearby castle of Invergarry, a place that will always be associated with an infamous feud. In 1663 the severed heads of seven murderers were presented to the chief of the clan, following an atrocity committed against one of his relatives.

LOCH HOPE, SUTHERLAND

Right: SITUATED IN A NORTH-WESTERN corner of the Highlands, Loch Hope is a narrow strip of water that almost reaches the sea. The area is sparsely inhabited, but there have been settlements here since prehistoric times. Chief among these was the Iron Age broch of Dornadilla, at the southern end of the loch. Perhaps because of its isolated position, this is unusually well preserved.

GLEN CONVINTH, INVERNESS

Right: THIS BEAUTIFUL GLEN lies just north-west of
Loch Ness, famed throughout the world for its monster.
Modern sightings date from the 1930s, but the tradition
is much older. In his 7th-century account, St Columba's
biographer described how the saint (*c.* 521–97)
confronted the fearsome sea beast, to save the life of a
monk who was swimming in the loch. In more recent
times, Glen Convinth became associated with the
Frasers of Lovat. They were of Norman stock and, in
1230, founded the nearby priory of Beauly. Their most
famous offspring was Simon Lovat (*c.* 1667–1747), the
'Old Fox of the '45', who was beheaded for his part in
the Jacobite rebellion.

GLAS BHEINN, SUTHERLAND

Above: THE CRAGGY HEIGHTS of Glas Bheinn ('grey mountain') are situated to the north of Loch Assynt, in an area that is rich in prehistoric associations. At the caves of Inchnadamph, traces have been found of animals from the Pleistocene era (*c.* 10,000 BC), among them the ancestors of reindeer, boar and the great Caledonian bear. Samples of Archaean gneiss rock – one of the oldest-known formations – were also noted.

EILEAN DONAN CASTLE, ROSS & CROMARTY

Right: BUILT ON THE SITE of an Iron Age fort, the present castle of Eilean Donan was constructed by Alexander II in 1220, as part of the region's defences against Viking attacks. It later passed into the hands of the MacKenzies of Kintail and subsequently became linked with the MacRae clan. Spanish troops were garrisoned there during the first Jacobite uprising (1715), when the castle was severely damaged by English warships.

LOCH MOIDART, INVERNESS

Right: THE COUNTRYSIDE around Loch Moidart was controlled by the MacDonalds of Clanranald. They were staunch supporters of Bonnie Prince Charlie, and encouraged him in his fateful bid for power. When he arrived on the Scottish mainland in July 1745, they offered him shelter at Kinlochmoidart House, together with his seven companions. After the failure of the rising this house was destroyed, but a row of beech trees (the 'Seven Men of Moidart') was later planted to commemorate the bravery of the prince's followers.

Cawdor Castle, Nairn

Right: THE CASTLE IS THE seat of the Thane of Cawdor, a
title immortalized in *Macbeth* (1606). In Shakespeare's
play this honour proved a mixed blessing, launching
Macbeth on his career of murder and tyranny. The real
Macbeth appears to have been rather less villainous. He
slew Duncan in battle in 1040, but ruled wisely in his
stead. One source even relates how he travelled to Rome
as a pilgrim, making generous donations to the poor and
needy. The present castle, dating from 1372, is located
1.6 km (1 mile) away from the original building.

GLENFINNAN, INVERNESS

Right: ON 19 AUGUST 1745 the standard of Bonnie Prince Charlie was raised at Glenfinnan, signalling the start of the second Jacobite rebellion. As the banner was being unfurled, the prince's father was proclaimed King James VIII of Scotland (James III of England). The initial response to the rising was disappointing but, with the support of the MacDonalds and the Camerons, it soon gathered momentum and the army marched south towards Edinburgh.

CLAN BURIAL STONE, CULLODEN, INVERNESS

Below: LESS THAN A YEAR later the Jacobite dream was over. On 16 April 1746 Prince Charles's forces were routed by the English army, in a battle lasting just 40 minutes. The consequences of this defeat were far-reaching, as the Highlanders' ancient way of life was swept away by the victors. Symbolic gravestones were later erected on the battlefield, commemorating the clans that had fought so hard and died for the Jacobite cause.

THE GATEWAY TO THE WEST

THE GAELIC-SPEAKING RACE known as the Scots made their first recorded appearance on the mainland in the early years of the 6th century. Originally they came from Ireland, where there was fierce inter-tribal rivalry. In *c.* AD 500 the Dál Riata tribe, a branch of the Scots, decided to migrate to Scotland (then called Alban). There they established the kingdom of Dalriada, choosing Dunadd (see p. 8) near Loch Crinan as their capital.

This venture was not as hazardous as it might sound. The distance between Antrim and Argyll was not great – as little as 19 km (12 miles) at its shortest point – and small parties had probably been making the crossing for many years. Besides, the tribe did not abandon its Irish base altogether.

LEFT: SUNSET AT CALLANISH, LEWIS

The stones at Callanish have always fuelled the imagination. Some believed the pillars were pagan chiefs, turned to stone for refusing to embrace the Christian faith.

ABOVE: CASTLE STALKER, ARGYLL

Situated on an island in Loch Linnhe, Castle Stalker has long been the stronghold of the Stewarts of Appin. It was built in c. 1500 and once served James IV as a hunting lodge.

The Scots soon prospered and were rapidly able to extend their territories. By the 7th century they held much of Argyll, from the Mull of Kintyre to Loch Moidart, along with many of the neighbouring isles. It is clear that, from the start, their strength was based on naval power. In 568 they undertook an expedition in the Hebrides, together with another Irish tribe. Then, in the 580s, Aedán, son of Gabran, launched attacks on both the Orkneys and the Isle of Man.

In spite of these forays, the nucleus of Dalriada consisted of three main regions, ruled by the descendants of Oenghus, Lorne and Gabran. Oenghus held Islay and Jura (and his distant offspring would eventually include Somerled, Lord of the Isles, and the clan MacDonald); Gabran took the land south of Loch Fyne; while Lorne occupied the area to the north.

Dalriada's Irish roots helped to change the face of western Scotland. In particular, they nurtured the spread of Christianity. In fact, the process of conversion had begun further south, but an influx of Irish monks in the 6th and 7th centuries gave it added momentum. St Moluag (c. 530–92) founded monasteries in Lismore, Skye and the outer Hebrides; Brendan of Clonfert (c. 486–c. 575) is said to have established a religious centre on the Firth of Lorne; and St Congan (8th century) led an expedition to Lochalsh, near Skye. But all these achievements paled beside the contribution of St Columba (c. 521–97).

Columba arrived in Iona in 563, together with 12 companions. There is a tale that he left Ireland under a cloud, after refusing to return a manuscript that he had been copying. The island was granted to him by Conall, King of Dalriada, in order that he might undertake the conversion of the Picts. Comparatively little is known of this mission, although Bridei (or Brude), the Pictish king, evidently gave permission for Columba and his monks to preach within his realm. In time, they built up a network of monasteries throughout Pictland (see pp. 95–7) and the West.

The prestige of Iona can also be gauged by the fact that it was acknowledged as a royal church in 574. In all, 48 kings were buried on the isle. This in turn led to an upsurge in artistic activity in the area. Mimicking the flowing Celtic styles from Ireland, local stone-carvers began to produce a fine array of monumental crosses (see p. 72) and grave-slabs. The best-known workshop was on Iona itself, but similar schools were set up at Islay, Oronsay and Loch Sween.

All too soon, however, the splendour of the monasteries began to attract the wrong sort of attention. In 795 a small Viking force landed on Iona, no doubt delighted to find a rich monastery that was totally undefended. Further raids followed, culminating in a brutal attack in 806, when 68 monks were killed. It was clear that Iona could no longer survive as the centre of the Columban order and many of the monks departed.

The strength of the Viking fleet soon gave them control over much of the West, a state of affairs that was to persist until King Haakon's defeat at the battle of Largs in 1263. As the Norsemen surged into their former territories, the Scots themselves pushed east into Pictish territory. In the early years of the 9th century they established a new capital at Forteviot. Then, in c. 843, they managed to unite the two lands under a single crown, when their leader, Kenneth MacAlpin, was accepted as King of the Picts. He is traditionally regarded as the first King of Scotland.

LEFT: BALLYMEANOCH, ARGYLL

These paired stones are part of the prehistoric complex in Kilmartin Valley. They are situated close to a henge, and carvings of cup-marks, arcs and grooved lines can be discerned on some of the stones.

FINGAL'S CAVE, STAFFA

Left and right: THE STRIKING BASALT columns that line Fingal's Cave were caused by a series of volcanic eruptions, running between Skye and the Irish coast. Similar rock formations were created elsewhere, most notably at the Giant's Causeway on the north coast of Ireland. Both these geological wonders were ascribed to the same legendary figure: the 3rd-century Irish warrior-hero, Finn MacCool, known in Scotland as Fingal and often portrayed as a giant. He was said to have built a magic bridge between Ireland and the Hebrides, so that he could visit his sweetheart in the Scottish isles.

KILCHOAN TOMB, ARGYLL

Above: THE PREHISTORIC GRAVE AT Kilchoan belongs to the Kilmartin group of monuments. Its shape
must have reminded later generations of a monk's retreat, for the name literally means 'the cell of
Congan'. The latter was the exiled son of an Irish chieftain, who became a missionary saint. He founded
the monastery of Lochalsh near Skye and was accorded the honour of burial on Iona.

CUP-AND-RING MARKS, KILMARTIN, ARGYLL

Above: THIS NETWORK OF BRONZE AGE carvings can be found at Cairnbaan, in the Kilmartin complex.
Similar designs have been noted in other parts of the British Isles and in north-west Spain. Their purpose
is uncertain: some believe they were magical sun symbols, aimed at summoning back the warmth of
summer; others regard them as prospectors' marks, boundary signs or even gaming boards.

THE STANDING STONES OF CALLANISH, LEWIS

Right: SOMETIMES DESCRIBED as Scotland's Stonehenge,
Callanish is laid out in a unique formation. At its core
there is a stone circle, with an avenue (a double line) of
stones leading north, and single lines leading east, west
and south. Within the circle, a chambered cairn and
central pillar-stone are jointly aligned, so that the latter's
shadow penetrates the tomb at the equinoxes. Callanish
is the focus of many legends, among them a belief that
the stones are the petrified victims ('the False Men' in
Gaelic) of Druid priests.

KILMARTIN VALLEY, ARGYLL

Right: THE IMPRESSIVE RANGE of prehistoric monuments in Kilmartin Valley makes this one of Scotland's most intriguing archaeological sites. Within the space of a few miles there are stone circles, burial cists, cairns, cup-and-ring marks and individual standing stones. At the spine of this grouping there is a linear cemetery, consisting of five cairns – Glebe cairn, the three Nether Largie cairns and Ri Cruin – dating back to the 2nd millennium BC. The twin standing stones at Carnasserie (left) may also have had a funerary aspect. Some paired stones had male and female (i.e. fertility) overtones, while others were placed on either side of a burial pit.

ARDCHATTAN PRIORY, ARGYLL

Left: A SCATTERING OF finely carved burial slabs offers a gloomy reminder of Ardchattan's former glories. The priory, which takes its name from St Cathan, was founded in 1230 for monks of the Valliscaulian order (an austere branch of the Benedictines). It proved sufficiently grand for Robert the Bruce to convene his parliament here in 1308 – the last one to be held in Gaelic – but the church was later burned by Cromwellian troops.

DUMBARTON ROCK AND CASTLE, DUNBARTONSHIRE

Right: DUMBARTON (LITERALLY 'the Fort of the Britons') holds a special place in Scottish history. From the 5th century it was the chief stronghold of the kingdom of Strathclyde, later becoming a royal castle. It has also been hailed by some as the birthplace of both St Gildas (*c.* 493–570) and St Patrick (389–*c.* 461). Indeed, one legend relates that the rock itself was hurled at St Patrick by a furious band of witches.

Kintraw, Argyll

Right: SITUATED AT THE head of Loch Craignish, the prehistoric site of Kintraw contains four cairns and a large standing stone. The latter rises to a height of 4 metres (13 feet) and is often cited in discussions about ancient observatories. From this viewpoint, the light of the setting sun at the midwinter solstice falls precisely in the notch between the twin peaks of Beinn Shiantaidh and Beinn á Chaolais, almost 48 km (30 miles) away on the island of Jura. Some experts believe the standing stone was deliberately positioned here, to provide a marking post for this phenomenon.

CASTLE DOUNIE, ARGYLL

Above: OVERLOOKING THE SHORES of Loch Crinan, this sturdy hillfort was probably built as a lookout post by the ancient Scots. It guarded the sea approach from Ireland and was ideal for relaying information to the stronghold of Dunadd, situated just a few miles to the east. These were important considerations in the pre-Viking period, when the two kingdoms of Dalriada maintained very close contact.

CASTLE SWEEN, ARGYLL

Above: PERCHED ON A ROCKY RIDGE, Castle Sween is often cited as the earliest stone castle in Scotland.
It dates from the 12th century and was built by the MacSweens (originally Sueno), a family of Norse
extraction. The castle was besieged by Robert the Bruce, who then installed the MacNeills as
Constables of Sween. It was eventually destroyed by the Royalists in 1647.

CELTIC CROSS, IONA

Left: IONA IS SCOTLAND'S holiest shrine. In 563 St Columba founded a monastery here, having been granted the island by Conall, the ruler of Dalriada. Through the saint's missionary zeal, Iona soon became the head of a large federation of Scottish and Irish monasteries. Its exposed position made it vulnerable to Viking attacks, however, and in the 9th century Iona's authority was transferred to Kells, in Ireland, and Dunkeld in Scotland.

FIONNPHORT, MULL

Right: JAGGED BOULDERS OF pink granite line the coast at Fionnphort, many of them split apart like broken teeth. This rocky spot on the west coast of Mull is the embarkation point for Iona, which lies just across the narrow sound that separates the two islands. For centuries Fionnphort has been the last stage on the old pilgrim route for visitors wishing to see the cradle of Scottish Christianity.

Clach Mhic Leoid, Harris

Right: Some of the standing stones in the Western Isles
blend so perfectly with their setting that it is tempting
to view them as integral parts of the landscape.
Nevertheless, it is possible that many sites were chosen
for very specific reasons. According to one theory, this
monolith near the Sound of Taransay belongs to a group
of four, which were carefully aligned with the peak of
Boreray on St Kilda. On important, seasonal dates, the
sun appears to set behind the mountain, when viewed
from the relevant stone.

THE CUILLINS, SKYE

Above: SKYE'S FAMOUS MOUNTAIN range attains heights of well over 915 metres (3,000 feet) and can be seen for miles around. The peaks used to be spelled in a variety of different ways, including Cuchullin. This has fuelled speculation that they were named after a legendary Irish hero, Cú Chulainn. Even today, the silhouette of the mountains is often likened to a giant, sleeping warrior.

RHUM & EIGG

Right: THIS VIEW IS TAKEN from the beach at Glenancross, just south of Mallaig. It looks across to Rhum and Eigg, two of the smaller islands in the Inner Hebrides. Eigg was a traditional seat of the MacDonalds, many of whose graves can still be seen at Kildonnan. Rhum is today inhabited by a strain of wild ponies, said to be descended from the stock of a shipwrecked Spanish galleon.

DUNVEGAN CASTLE, SKYE

Above: DUNVEGAN CASTLE HAS BEEN the seat of the MacLeods for at least 800 years. The oldest part of the present structure is probably the keep, which dates from the 14th century, while the 'Fairy Tower' was added in the 16th century. This takes its picturesque name from a magical flag, given to one of the ancient MacLeods by a fairy lover and said to have the power to rescue clan members from danger.

THE STORR, SKYE

Above: THE STORR IS A FREAKISH RIDGE of basalt pinnacles, rising out of the Trotternish peninsula. The largest of the pillars, which reaches a height of 49 metres (160 feet), is known as the Old Man of Storr. Near its base, a hoard of treasure was discovered in 1891, consisting mainly of jewellery and 10th-century coins. It is thought to have been hidden there by a Viking raider.

Loch Lomond, Dunbartonshire

Right: THIS BEAUTIFUL STRETCH of water is famed for the ballad *The Bonnie Banks of Loch Lomond*, which begins with the lines: 'Oh, ye'll take the high road, An' I'll take the low road, An' I'll be in Scotland afore ye'. But behind these innocent-sounding lyrics lies a tragic story. For the composer was Donald MacDonald of Keppoch, a Jacobite soldier condemned to death after the battle of Culloden (1746). In his case, 'the low road' hinted at his imminent execution, for there was an old belief that the spirits of the dead returned to their homeland beneath the earth.

KILCHURN CASTLE, LOCH AWE, ARGYLL

Left: THE POWERFUL KEEP of Kilchurn Castle was erected in *c.* 1440 by Sir Colin Campbell of Glenorchy. For three centuries it offered protection to his descendants, the Campbells of Breadalbane, before falling into Hanoverian hands. Impressive as it is, Kilchurn is surrounded by much older fortifications. When the waters are low, traces of crannogs (prehistoric island dwellings) can be seen in the loch.

RIVER ARAY, ARGYLL

Right: THE ARAY, WHICH extends from Loch Fyne to Loch Awe, lies deep in the heart of Campbell country. This famous clan was founded in the 13th century by Cailean Mor ('Great Colin') and one of its chief strongholds, the castle of Inverary, can be found at the mouth of the river, where it flows into Loch Fyne.

GLEN LUSS, DUNBARTONSHIRE

Right: THE GENTLE SLOPES of Glen Luss run west from
Loch Lomond. The people of this area were converted
by St Kessog, a 6th-century Irish monk. His cult
remained strong for many centuries and the church of
Luss, where Kessog was buried, was granted the status of
a sanctuary by Robert the Bruce. Prior to this, the glen
came under threat from one of the most daring Viking
raids. In 1263, 60 of King Haakon's longships sailed up
Loch Long and were then hauled overland to Loch
Lomond. There, the Norsemen proceeded to ravage
much of the surrounding countryside.

EARLY CHRISTIAN CROSSES, KEILLS, ARGYLL

Below: THROUGH ITS CLOSE cultural links with its western neighbour, Dalriada imported many features of Irish art. The influence of stone-carving was particularly strong, with the result that Argyll and the Hebrides produced the finest Celtic crosses in Scotland. These examples, created for a monastery that has long since vanished, may date from as early as the 8th century.

LOCH CRINAN, ARGYLL

Right: THESE TRANQUIL WATERS lie very close to the heart of ancient Dalriada. When the Scots migrated here in the early 6th century, they established their capital at nearby Dunadd. Because of their continuing connections with Ulster, they needed a site that was close to the coast, and the short passage along the River Add and Loch Crinan gave them ready access to the open sea.

KILDALTON CHURCH, ISLAY

Left: THE CELTIC CROSS at Kildalton (detail) is one of the most impressive examples in the country. Standing 2.7 metres (9 feet) high, it was cut from a single slab of stone and was probably completed in the early 9th century. The decoration maintains a careful balance between winding tendril patterns and tiny scenes taken from the Scriptures. Preserved in the churchyard are also a number of early grave-slabs, among them this figure of a medieval knight (right). The ultimate inspiration for such carvings came from Iona, where generations of kings and chieftains lay buried under elaborate effigies.

Innis Chonnell Castle, Argyll

Right: Situated on Loch Awe, the island castle of Innis Chonnell has left its mark on history as one of the earliest strongholds of the Campbell clan. The family secured its grip on the region in the 13th century, when Archibald Campbell acquired the lordship of Lochow (or Lochawe), through his marriage to the daughter of the royal treasurer. Innis Chonnell itself was initially designed as a 'castle of enclosure' (a simple courtyard enclosed within a curtain wall), but its living apartments were later improved.

KILNEUAIR, ARGYLL

Below: A FEW CRUMBLING fragments are all that remain of this ancient church, which stands at the southern end of Loch Awe. It is dedicated to St Columba, though it is unclear whether the saint had any specific connections with the place. Little is known of his missions on the Scottish mainland, apart from the fact that he journeyed to Pictland, to convert Bridei, son of Maelchon.

CRANNOG, LOCH AWE, ARGYLL

Right: CRANNOGS, SUCH AS this one on Loch Awe, are one of the oldest-known forms of defensive structure. Usually found on lakes or marshy ground, they are essentially artificial islands, built up from layers of peat, stones and logs. Crowning this would normally have been a single, timber hut. The idea originated in prehistoric times, but some crannogs stayed in use until the early medieval period.

THE KINGDOM OF
THE PICTS

T HE NORTH-EAST HAS LONG been regarded as
the heartland of the Picts, that mysterious
race which formed the backbone of ancient
Scotland. They created a nation of sorts, uniting
various different tribes under a common cause, and
their surviving artworks suggest a well-developed,
individual culture. Despite this, their early history
remains tantalizingly unclear.

The earliest factual information stems from the
Roman invasion of the North. In the course of his
campaigns (AD 79–84), Agricola noted a number of
different tribes and these were later recorded on
Ptolemy's map of the area (see p. 136). The most
prominent of these peoples were the Caledonii or
Caledonians, whose name was sometimes used

LEFT: DUNNOTTAR CASTLE, KINCARDINE

*Spectacularly situated on a rocky promontory, Dunnottar has
had a castle since Pictish times. Franco Zeffirelli used this as a
location in his film version of* Hamlet.

ABOVE: EDINBURGH CASTLE, MIDLOTHIAN

Many kings have made use of Edinburgh's strong defensive position. Edwin of Northumbria (c. 585–633) had a stronghold here, as did Malcolm Canmore four centuries later. The oldest part is St Margaret's Chapel, dating from 1076.

loosely to describe all the northern tribes. They were also specified as the defeated tribe at the battle of Mons Graupius (AD 84), where, it is said, 10,000 warriors were lost.

In 297 a new name appeared in historical accounts. For the first time, a Roman writer talked of the *Picti* ('the Painted Ones'), who lived in the far north. This term did not imply the arrival of a new tribe; it simply referred to the warriors' practice of painting or tattooing their exposed areas of skin. The name

quickly caught on and, during the 4th century, reports of Pictish raids into the Lowlands and beyond became ever more frequent. These attacks were still continuing when the Romans finally withdrew from Britain in 410.

The origins of the Picts are a matter of controversy, partly because of a lack of hard information and partly because of the conflicting legends that are associated with them. In the 8th century, for example, Bede claimed that they came from Scythia. This notion probably stemmed from a garbled version of the legend of St Andrew, for a similar story was also told about the Scots (see p. 118). Equally, another long-held view was that the Picts arrived in Scotland with no wives and that these were granted to them by the Irish, on the understanding that the right of succession would run through the female line. Again, this was undoubtedly a later invention, used by commentators to explain away the Picts' unusual inheritance rules.

The Picts themselves described their origins in terms of a genealogical table. In a manuscript of the *Pictish Chronicle*, thought to date back to the 10th century, they identified the father of their race as a king named Cruithne. He had seven sons – Fib, Fidach, Fotlaig, Fortrenn, Cait, Ce and Circinn – and divided up his lands between them. These names are now thought to refer to seven early kingdoms, rather than individual people. Thus, Fib stands for Fife; Cait for Caithness; and Fotlaig may be an early form of Atfolda (the old name for Atholl).

Modern authorities tend towards the view that the Picts were a Celtic people, who migrated to Scotland during the Iron Age, perhaps in around 500 BC. There is no way of knowing if there ever were seven Pictish kingdoms but, by the Roman period, there seems to have been a general distinction between the northern and southern Picts, with the Grampians forming a natural barrier between the two. The full extent of their rule is uncertain, but it is clear that there were substantial Pictish settlements in the Orkneys (see pp. 28 and 29). There are also hints that the Dalriadan Scots established their colony in territory that was nominally held by the Picts. So, at one time or another, it is possible that the Picts held sway over most of the land north of Strathclyde.

Their fortunes come into sharper focus during the early Christian period. Some sources claim that St Ninian made converts among the southern Picts and that in *c.* 486 Darlugdach, Abbess of Kildare, founded a church at Abernethy, in Perthshire. But the first undisputed mission was led by St Columba, who gained an audience with King Bridei (or Brude) in *c.* 563. The latter was evidently a very powerful figure. In his 30-year reign (*c.* 554–84) he won a resounding victory against Dalriada (560) and was strong enough to exact hostages from his subjects in the Orkneys. Towards the end of his life he had the distinction of uniting the northern and southern Picts under his rule.

Such unity was vital for, in the following century, Pictish territory came under

increasing threat from the Angles of Northumbria. They swept aside the Border tribes, captured Fife and made rapid inroads beyond the Tay. Eventually, though, their progress was brought to a dramatic halt near Forfar, at the battle of Nechtansmere (685). Egfrith, the Northumbrian king, was killed, along with much of his army. After this, the Anglian menace receded.

The 8th century marked the height of Pictish power. In 736 Oenghus (728–61) invaded Dalriada, capturing Dunadd and deposing the Scottish king. Then, for a brief, glorious spell, the Picts were masters of all the land above the Forth–Clyde line. This feat was repeated by one of Oenghus's successors, Constantine (ruled *c.* 782–*c.* 818), although the last years of his reign were marred by the onset of the Viking raids. Ironically, the gradual merging of the two rival kingdoms signalled the end of Pictish power. For the next leader to rule over them both was the Scottish king, Kenneth MacAlpin, who assumed the throne in *c.* 843. After this, the concept of a separate Pictish kingdom rapidly melted away.

LEFT: CROSS-SLAB, ABERLEMNO, ANGUS

This Pictish cross stands by an ancient track, which led from the fort of Finavon to the monastery at Brechin. Beneath the huge wheel of the cross, two angels bow their heads in contemplation.

BALBIRNIE STONE CIRCLE, FIFE

Right: MANY PREHISTORIC SITES were altered and re-used
by succeeding generations. At Balbirnie the ancient
stone circle was transformed, when a later race of people
placed a series of cist-graves within the enclosure. Some
of these had cup-marks on their flanking stones and can
be dated to around 1330 BC. A few appear to have been
reserved for cremation burials of women and children.
During Balbirnie's final phase (*c.* 890 BC), a low cairn
was heaped on top of the cists and fragments of cremated
bone were scattered over the boulders.

FORTINGALL, PERTHSHIRE

Above: THERE IS NO SHORTAGE OF antiquities at Fortingall: a cup-marked stone; a 2,000-year-old yew tree; an arrangement of standing stones, set in groups of three (above); and the remains of an Iron Age ring-fort. Most curious of all is the story that Pontius Pilate was born here, the son of a Roman envoy to a local chieftain.

WATLING LODGE, ANTONINE WALL, STIRLING

Above: BUILT IN C. AD 143–4, the Antonine Wall stretched for some
60 km (37 miles) along the Forth–Clyde isthmus. Large stretches
were protected by a substantial ditch, 12 metres (40 feet) wide and
3.7 metres (12 feet) deep. Part of this can still be seen at Watling
Lodge, midway between Falkirk and Rough Castle.

Loch Muick, Aberdeenshire

Left: FEW PLACES IN SCOTLAND can rival the spectacular scenery of Loch Muick. Lying just to the south of Balmoral Forest and overshadowed by the heights of Lochnagar, it has been admired by royalty and poets, by ornithologists and climbers. Initially, the main authority in the region came from the Gordons, a Border clan who moved to Aberdeenshire in the 14th century. Latterly, the area became a favourite with the Royal Family, particularly after the purchase of the Balmoral estate in 1852. Sixteen years later, Queen Victoria built a lodge at the edge of Loch Muick, nicknamed the 'Widow's House', because she used it as a retreat during her long period of mourning.

ROUGH CASTLE, ANTONINE WALL, STIRLING

Below: THE APPEARANCE OF the Antonine Wall was much less imposing than that of its southern equivalent, Hadrian's Wall. In place of stone, much of the barrier was composed of turf ramparts, ditches and other earthworks. Rough Castle, located near the eastern end of the wall, has some of the best-preserved examples of these fortifications. Here, the hollows in the foreground are defence-pits, nicknamed *lilia* (lilies) by Roman soldiers.

CULLERLIE STONE CIRCLE, ABERDEENSHIRE

Right: THIS UNUSUAL MONUMENT consists of a small circle, 9.7 metres (32 feet) in diameter, formed by eight boulders. Within the circle there are seven tiny cairns, the largest of them positioned in the centre. The contents have been looted, but the cairns were probably used for cremation burials. Indeed, it has been suggested that the central cairn belonged to a chief, while the satellite tombs were for his dependants, ritually slain at the time of his death.

Easter Aquhorthies, Inverurie, Aberdeenshire

Right: THIS IS A FINE EXAMPLE OF a recumbent stone circle – a circle where the 'entrance' to the ring is marked by a massive horizontal stone, flanked by two tall portal stones. In this, as in other similar monuments, the entrance is sited in the south-western quadrant of the circle. A distinction can also be made between the granite of the entry stones and the pinkish porphyry of the remaining boulders. Early commentators interpreted the horizontal stone as a pagan altar, but its true purpose remains uncertain.

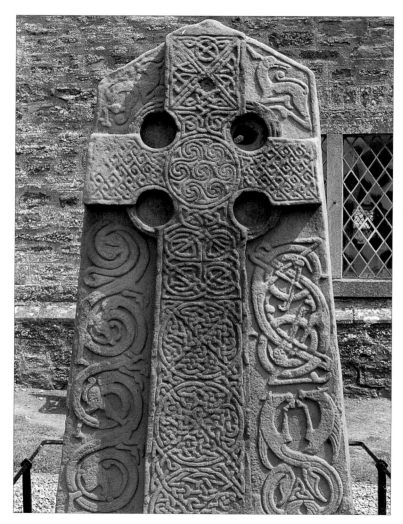

CROSS-SLAB, ABERLEMNO, ANGUS

Left and right: THREE PICTISH STONES have survived at the village of Aberlemno: a tilting pillar covered in enigmatic symbols and two cross-slabs. These details come from the older of the two slabs, which probably dates from the 8th century. On one side, it bears a Celtic cross, carved in high-relief and set against a background of interlacing, snake-like monsters. On the reverse, a pitched battle between helmeted and bare-headed warriors is shown. This may represent the battle of Nechtansmere, where the Picts had won their famous victory over the Angles. The battlefield was just a few miles away from Aberlemno, and surviving Anglian helmets, with their long nose-guards, are similar to those portrayed on the stone.

Stonehaven, Kincardine

Right: IN COMMON WITH Burghead and Lerwick,
Stonehaven is the setting for a mid-winter fire festival,
which does little to disguise its pagan roots. At the
stroke of New Year, groups of youths parade along the
High Street whirling fireballs – paraffin-soaked rags in
mesh containers – in the night air. These are intended
to dispel evil spirits and ensure the prosperity of the
fishermen. Burghead's festival is known as 'Burning the
Clavie' (a tar-barrel), while the Shetlanders celebrate
'Up-Helly-Aa'. This culminates in the spectacle of a
Viking longship being drawn through the town
and then set alight.

BRECHIN ROUND TOWER, ANGUS

Right: ROUND TOWERS WERE ERECTED as lookout points for early churches. They were extremely common in ancient Ireland, but rare in Scotland. Only two examples have survived on the mainland. Brechin's tower is the oldest and is thought to have been built by Irish masons in the late 10th or early 11th century. For reasons of security, the narrow doorway (left) was set high above the ground – 1.8 metres (6 feet) above in this instance – and had to be reached by a ladder. The moulding around the door is unusually ornate, with a Crucifixion on the lintel and two figures of Culdee churchmen on either side.

DUNNOTTAR CASTLE, KINCARDINE

Right: THE PICTS BUILT A CASTLE at Dunnottar, perhaps the *Dun Fother* that is mentioned prominently in several of the early annals. Legend has it that there was also an early Christian chapel, dedicated to St Ninian. The present ruins belong to a series of fortifications, erected here between the 12th and 14th centuries. Among these was the castle, which William Wallace took from the English in 1297. This was superseded by the stronghold of 1392, built by Sir William Keith, Earl Marischal of Scotland. Dunnottar remained an important base until the days of the Civil War (1642–9), when the Scottish regalia were held here for safe-keeping.

ARBROATH ABBEY, ANGUS

Left: THIS ABBEY HOLDS A SPECIAL PLACE in Scottish history, for it was here that supporters of Robert the Bruce signed the Declaration of Arbroath in 1320. This famous document, which amounted to a declaration of independence, was probably drawn up by the abbot of Arbroath, Bernard de Linton, and was then despatched to Pope John XXII. The abbey itself (originally a priory) was founded in 1178 by William the Lion (1143–1214). The rose window (left), known locally as 'the O of Arbroath', was illuminated, to act as a primitive lighthouse. The carved figures (above) are from the tomb chest of Abbot Paniter.

DUNFERMLINE ABBEY, FIFE

Left: IN 1067 MALCOLM CANMORE (ruled 1058–93) married Margaret, his saintly Saxon princess, at Dunfermline. Shortly afterwards, she founded a Benedictine priory here, sending to England for monks who would help reform the Celtic Church. St Margaret's shrine would later make Dunfermline a place of pilgrimage, but she was not the only worthy to be buried here. Robert the Bruce was also interred in the abbey. His grave was uncovered by accident in 1818, when workmen found a skeleton with saw-marks on its breastbone, showing where the heart had been removed (see pp. 146–7).

ST ANDREWS CATHEDRAL, FIFE

Right: ST ANDREWS OWES ITS name to an ancient legend, which claimed that the apostle's bones were transported here by St Rule in the 4th century and buried on the site of the present cathedral. This same tradition also argued that the Scottish race originated in Scythia, the very area that had been evangelized by St Andrew. It was for this reason that he was chosen as Scotland's patron saint.

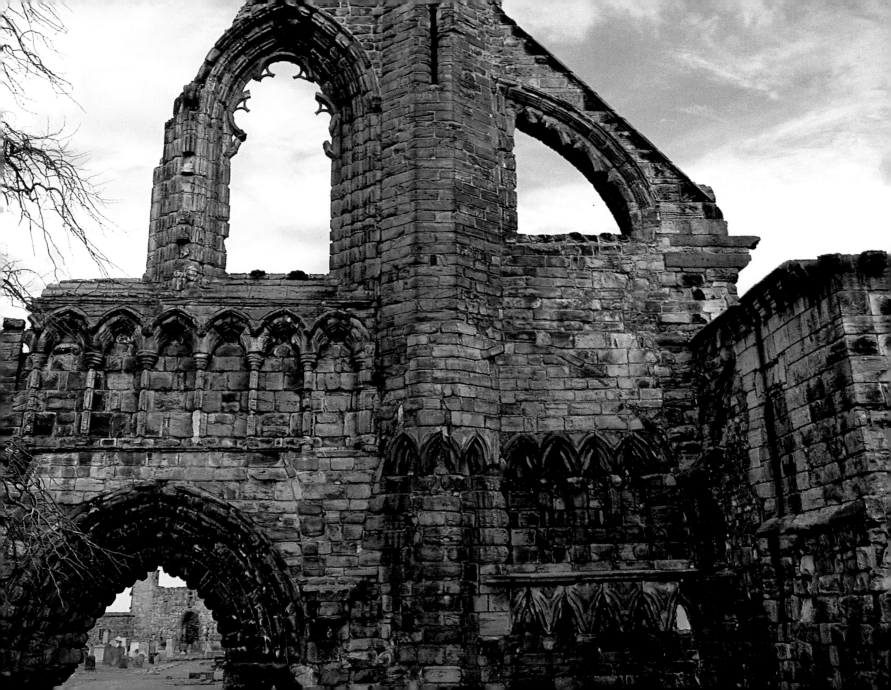

THE BASS, INVERURIE, ABERDEENSHIRE

Below: THE SOLE REMINDER OF Inverurie's castle is an imposing, 18-metre (60-foot) mound, known locally as the Bass. This was erected in 1160 by the Lord of Garloch, as a platform for a wooden tower. Later there was a stone castle on the site. The adjoining churchyard is of even greater antiquity, for several of its memorial slabs are carved with Pictish symbols.

DIRLETON CASTLE, EAST LOTHIAN

Right: OVERLOOKING AN IMPORTANT coastal route, Dirleton's castle dates back to the 13th century. It was built by the de Vaux, a prominent Anglo-Norman family, and the first real test of its defences came in 1298, when it was besieged by Edward I's forces. Later additions to the castle were made by the Halyburtons and the Ruthvens, before it was destroyed by Cromwellian troops.

FALLS OF DOCHART, PERTHSHIRE

Right: THE TUMBLING WATERS of the River Dochart course through a region called Breadalbane. Several clans competed for supremacy here, among them the Campbells, the MacNabs, the MacGregors and the MacLarens. The MacNabs claimed the most ancient connections with the area, stressing their descent from the abbots of Glendochart. Their traditional burial ground lies on a tiny island, Inch Buie, which is situated just below the Falls of Dochart. In the 17th century, however, the Campbells gained ascendancy, when Sir John Campbell was created Earl of Breadalbane. This branch of the family is still known as the Campbells of Breadalbane.

DRUM CASTLE, ABERDEENSHIRE

Below: THE CONTRASTING STYLES of Drum Castle illustrate the changing needs of Highland lords. The massive, granite tower dates from the 13th century and was built as a royal stronghold. In 1323 Robert the Bruce gave it to his armour-bearer, William de Irwin, an ancestor of the Irvines. They added the elegant, baronial mansion (1619), which belongs to a rather more leisurely age.

STIRLING CASTLE, STIRLING

Right: STIRLING CASTLE'S ANCIENT links with the Scottish monarchy are well established. Alexander I died there in 1124 and the castle was later used as ransom to pay for the release of William the Lion. More notable still are the two famous victories fought within view of its ramparts. At Stirling Bridge (1297) Wallace routed the English, while Bruce achieved his greatest success at Bannockburn (1314).

DETAIL OF STATUARY, HOLYROOD PALACE, MIDLOTHIAN

Left: THE NAME HOLYROOD DERIVES from a relic of the True Cross, owned by Queen (later St) Margaret (*c.* 1046–93). Her son, David I, founded Holyrood Abbey in 1128 and its guest house eventually formed the nucleus of the palace. This is most closely associated with Mary Queen of Scots (1542–87), who lived here for a turbulent six years. During this time she married both Lord Darnley and the Earl of Bothwell, and witnessed the murder of her private secretary, David Rizzio.

JOHN KNOX'S HOUSE, EDINBURGH, MIDLOTHIAN

Above: FORMING PART OF THE ROYAL MILE, Knox's House dates from the late 15th century and retains its external stairway. Knox (*c.* 1502–72) was a Protestant Reformer, a firebrand with a vehement distrust of Catholics and women. His links with the house are uncertain, though it is claimed that he lived here from 1561 until his death.

LESLIE CASTLE, ABERDEENSHIRE

Right: AN INSCRIPTION CONFIRMS that this elegant castle was built in 1661, making it one of the last fortified houses in Scotland. There are a number of defensive features, but the overall impression is of a grand baronial residence, rather than a fortress. The basic plan of the building is L-shaped, with a protruding stair-tower. Not surprisingly, the castle was the preserve of the Leslie clan. Their presence in Aberdeenshire can be traced back to the 12th century, when their ancestor, a Flemish nobleman named Bartholomew, was granted the Barony of Lesly.

ROSSLYN CHAPEL, MIDLOTHIAN

Left: ROSSLYN'S GEM OF A CHAPEL was founded in 1446 by William Sinclair, 3rd Earl of Orkney. It is justly celebrated for its wealth of delicate carvings, among them the figure of an angel playing the bagpipes (right). Finest of all is the so-called Apprentice Pillar (left), which was supposedly made by a young trainee. His master was so jealous of this that he killed the apprentice and, in commemoration, a portrait of the victim – complete with a scar on his brow – was added to the decoration in the church. The story has an air of fiction about it, although it is known that the chapel had to be re-consecrated, because some terrible act had been committed within its walls.

Tantallon Castle, East Lothian

Right: THIS ROSE-COLOURED RUIN is perched on a rocky shelf above the Firth of Forth. For centuries it was a stronghold of the Douglas clan and had the reputation of being impregnable. This held true until 1651, when Cromwellian forces stormed the castle, after bombarding it with artillery for a full 12 days. In the background, the Bass Rock appears scarcely less imposing. St Baldred is said to have built a hermitage here in the 7th century, but the place became better known as a fortress and prison. In particular, Charles II used it for the confinement of Covenanters (rebellious Scottish Presbyterians).

THE BASTION AGAINST THE SOUTH

THE INHABITANTS OF ancient Scotland had to fend off threats of attack or invasion from almost every quarter. Throughout much of their early history, however, the greatest menace came from the south. In the first centuries after Christ, the principal enemy was Rome. In AD 79 Gnaeus Julius Agricola (AD 40–93), governor of the province of Britain, launched an invasion of the North with the Ninth Legion. He rapidly penetrated as far as the River Tay, erecting a number of forts on the Forth–Clyde isthmus to consolidate his position. Then, in AD 84, he pushed further north, winning a decisive victory over Calgacus, the Caledonian chief, at Mons Graupius, somewhere deep in the Highlands, perhaps near Stonehaven.

LEFT: EILDON HILLS, ROXBURGH

Site of an ancient hillfort and Roman signal station, the Eildons' most enduring associations are with Thomas the Rhymer, subject of a famous romance telling of his journey with the Queen of Faeries to an enchanted land beneath the hills.

ABOVE: CAIRNHOLY CHAMBERED CAIRN, KIRKCUDBRIGHT

This is a court cairn, consisting of a burial chamber (foreground) and a crescent-shaped line of stones. Inside, archaeologists recovered a ceremonial axe and shards of neolithic pottery.

Agricola was recalled to Rome in AD 85, and the most advanced bases were soon abandoned. When Hadrian's Wall came to be built (*c.* 122–8), the Roman border had shifted considerably to the south. But Agricola's campaigns ensured that the Lowlands were better documented than other parts of Scotland. This enabled Ptolemy, the 2nd-century geographer, to include several tribes and place-names in his map of the area. Details were fleshed out by the historian Tacitus (*c.* 55–120).

From Tacitus, it seems clear that there were four main tribes in the Border region: the Damnonii, the Novantae, the Selgovae and the Votadini. The Damnonii held sway in the area around the Clyde basin, eventually emerging as the Britons of Strathclyde. Their kingdom, centred on Dumbarton Rock, retained its independence until the Anglo-Norman period.

The Novantae were located in the south-west, in Galloway and Dumfries. They formed the nucleus of the kingdom of Rheged, which reached its peak in the 6th century, and appear to have taken control of such places as Carlisle. The Selgovae (literally 'Hunters') are much more obscure. Little is known about them, apart from the fact that they congregated to the east, in the Tweed basin.

The best-known tribe of the quartet were the Votadini, who occupied the Lothian area. They established strongholds at Stirling and Din Eidyn (later to be the site of Edinburgh Castle), and extended their territories as far south as the Tyne. Eventually they formed the kingdom of Gododdin.

Relations between these four tribes and the Romans were often peaceful, and it has been suggested that they became *foederati* (vassals) of the Empire. Certainly they lived in an uncomfortable buffer-zone, separating the Romans from the Picts and the Caledonians. This zone was often under Roman control for, after the completion of Hadrian's Wall, the legions soon pushed north again. Under Antoninus Pius (86–161), southern Scotland was reoccupied and a second wall – duly named the Antonine Wall – was constructed (*c.* 143–4), on the Forth–Clyde isthmus.

The Roman period coincided with the introduction of Christianity. Here, the leading figures were Ninian, Kentigern and Cuthbert. The ministry of St Ninian (*fl.* 390–400) was most successful in Galloway, where he founded the church of Whithorn (see p. 149), though he was also said to have made converts among the southern Picts. St Kentigern (or Mungo, *c.* 518–603) concentrated on the Strathclyde region and, in the late 6th century, established religious centres at Hoddom and Glasgow. Through the latter he exercised spiritual authority over a wide area, extending south into Cumbria. St Cuthbert (*c.* 634–87) is principally associated with Lindisfarne in Northumbria, but his influence was also felt in Scotland. He was prior of Melrose (see pp. 146–7) in *c.* 661 and there was a shrine to him at Kirkcudbright (literally the 'church of Cuthbert'), which claimed to house his bones.

After the departure of the Romans, the Lowland tribes were menaced by a new invader, a Germanic people known as the Angles. They rapidly established the kingdoms of Bernicia and Deira, governed from Bamburgh and York respectively, which merged to form Northumbria in 605. From this powerful base, the Angles launched a wave of attacks into southern Scotland, swiftly subduing both Rheged and Gododdin. This inspired Scotland's earliest example of patriotic literature, a heroic poem called the *Gododdin* (*c.* 600). Anglian progress into the Borders was remorseless. Edinburgh fell in 638, and the presence of Anglian carvings at Ruthwell (see p. 148) and Jedburgh (see p. 142) underlines their growing influence. Only with the Pictish victory at Nechtansmere (685) was their advance halted.

ABOVE: JEDBURGH ABBEY, ROXBURGH

Jedburgh is notable for its ancient carvings, many of which were incorporated into the fabric of the abbey. These include a Roman altar slab, an early shrine and a tomb made out of an Anglian cross-shaft.

The Angles, of course, eventually became the English and, in this guise, continued to harass the Border Scots. Evidence of their ongoing hostility can be found in the many fortified houses and castles in the region. Despite this, there were times when the gulf between these traditional enemies was bridged. The reign of David I (1124–53), for example, witnessed the gradual absorption of the Lowlands into the Anglo-Norman sphere of influence and the endowing of the great Border abbeys.

TORHOUSEKIE STONE CIRCLE, WIGTOWNSHIRE

Above: THIS BRONZE AGE CIRCLE CONSISTS OF 19 granite boulders, set upon a man-made platform
of earth. It can probably be linked with a number of neighbouring, three-stone rows. One of these
rows – a pair of large stones flanking a smaller one – is located inside the circle.

TORHOUSEKIE OUTLYING STONES, WIGTOWNSHIRE

Above: ANOTHER THREE-STONE ROW AT Torhousekie stands 91 metres (100 yards) to the east of the stone circle, while a third was recorded in 1896, but has since vanished. Three-stone rows, most common in south-west Scotland, are sometimes interpreted as solar sightlines, as used by prehistoric astronomers.

HADRIAN'S WALL, NEAR STEEL RIGG, NORTHUMBERLAND

Right: HADRIAN'S WALL WAS one of the most remarkable feats of Roman engineering. Stretching for 117 km (73 miles) and reaching heights of around 6 metres (20 feet), the bulk of the wall was completed in just six years (*c*. AD 122–8). Rome's first invasion of the North (AD 79) had penetrated considerably further, as far as the Forth–Clyde isthmus, but troubles elsewhere in the Roman Empire soon forced it to abandon some of its most northerly forts. More than a simple border, the wall may also have been designed to separate the strongest northern tribes, to prevent them from uniting against Rome. The remains of the ancient border are now found in Northern England.

JEDBURGH ABBEY, ROXBURGH

Below: RECORDS SHOW THAT a church existed on this site in the 9th century. Then, in *c.* 1118, David I established a priory at Jedburgh, which was served by Augustinian canons from the French abbey of Beauvais. David's priory was upgraded to an abbey in 1147, even though its construction was not fully completed until the 13th century.

SWEETHEART ABBEY, KIRKCUDBRIGHT

Right: SWEETHEART ABBEY WAS FOUNDED in 1273 by Devorguilla, the mother of John Balliol, King of the Scots (ruled 1292–6). In later life, Devorguilla's dearest possession was the embalmed heart of her late husband, her 'sweet, silent companion', which she kept in an ivory casket. After her death, it was buried alongside her, giving the abbey its romantic name.

DRYBURGH ABBEY, BERWICKSHIRE

Left: DRYBURGH ABBEY STANDS on the site of an early Christian sanctuary, dedicated to St Modan, a 6th-century missionary. The abbey itself was founded in *c.* 1152 by Hugh de Morville, Constable of Scotland, and was occupied by Premonstratensian monks. They belonged to an 'open' order, a reformed branch of the Augustinians that was allowed to go out and preach in the community. Dryburgh was sacked by the English on several occasions, but much of the cloister has survived, along with a number of fine carvings (such as Adam and Eve, right). Sir Walter Scott (1771–1832) lies buried amid the ruins of Dryburgh Abbey.

Melrose Abbey, Roxburgh

Right: THE EARLIEST FOUNDATION at Melrose dates back to at least the 7th century, for Bede mentions that St Cuthbert trained here. The present abbey was established by David I in 1136, for the use of Cistercian monks from Rievaulx Abbey in Yorkshire. It was badly damaged by the English in 1322, though Robert the Bruce restored it four years later. Legend has it that his embalmed heart was later buried here, within the abbey precincts. A similar claim is made for the body of Michael Scot the Wizard (*c.* 1175–*c.* 1230).

RUTHWELL CROSS, DUMFRIES

Left: DATING FROM THE EARLY 8th century, the Ruthwell Cross is one of the chief masterpieces of Anglian sculpture. It features a number of Biblical scenes, among them this elegant portrayal of Mary Magdalene washing Christ's feet. Framing these images are extracts from a famous contemporary poem, *The Dream of the Rood*, inscribed in runic characters.

WHITHORN PRIORY, WIGTOWNSHIRE

Right: OFTEN DESCRIBED AS THE cradle of Scottish Christianity, this is the place where St Ninian began his missionary work. After studying in Rome, Ninian returned to his homeland and built his first church here in *c.* 397. This was a stone building covered in white plaster, known as the White House (*Huit Aern* in Anglo-Saxon, later corrupted to Whithorn). The 12th-century priory was run by Premonstratensian monks.

CAERLAVEROCK CASTLE, DUMFRIES

Above: IT IS NO ACCIDENT THAT Caerlaverock lies close to the remains of Iron Age and Roman forts, since it occupies a commanding strategic position, overlooking a narrow stretch of the Solway Firth. The castle itself dates from *c.* 1290 and features a unique triangular design. It has been the scene of many conflicts, most notably the siege of 1300, when 60 defenders held off an English force of 3,000 men for two days.

SMAILHOLM TOWER, ROXBURGH

Right: THIS IS A 16TH-CENTURY PEEL TOWER, a type of fortified dwelling that was common in the Borders. The watchman's seat and fire recess on the parapet emphasize that the occupants were always prepared for trouble. At one point, the tower was threatened with demolition, but the owner agreed to save it, if Sir Walter Scott would make it the subject of a ballad. He obliged, composing *The Eve of St John* for this purpose.

Clatteringshaws Loch, Kirkcudbright

Right: PEACEFUL THOUGH IT MAY LOOK, this district was the focus of Robert the Bruce's guerrilla campaign against the English, in the days when he was a fugitive from Edward I's soldiers. Bruce's Stone, located on the eastern shores of the lake, marks the site of the battle of Rapploch Moss, one of several victories achieved in 1307. A few miles to the west, at Loch Trool, there is a similar stone, commemorating the spot where Bruce and his companions harassed the enemy, by rolling boulders down upon them.

GLENLUCE ABBEY, WIGTOWNSHIRE

Above: ROLAND, EARL OF GALLOWAY, FOUNDED an imposing Cistercian abbey at Glenluce in 1190.
Little remains of his original edifice although, amidst the crumbling masonry, parts of the 15th-century
chapter house (ceiling detail of Green Man, right) and the medieval plumbing system have survived intact.
Folklorists insist that a darker treasure also lurks in the vicinity, for Michael Scot, the 13th-century wizard,
is said to have rescued the monks of Glenluce from an attack of the plague. Using his mystical powers, he
lured the plague-demon into a secret vault and trapped it there, leaving it to starve to death.

THREAVE CASTLE, KIRKCUDBRIGHT

Right: BUILT BY THE APTLY named Archibald the Grim,
3rd Earl of Douglas, Threave's forbidding tower stands
on an island in the River Dee. One of its most gruesome
features is a projecting stone above the entrance, which
is known as the 'Gallows Knob'. With chilling pride, its
owners used to boast that this 'never wanted for a tassel'.
Threave Castle remained a Douglas stronghold until
1455, when James II (1430–60) waged his war against
the clan. It was the last of their castles to fall,
succumbing only when the mighty cannon,
Mons Meg, was brought against it.

CHRONOLOGY

AD 79	Agricola's invasion of the North
AD 84	Battle of Mons Graupius
c. 122–8	Building of Hadrian's Wall
c. 143–4	Construction of the Antonine Wall
209	Campaign of Emperor Septimius Severus
297	First documented reference to the Picts
c. 397	St Ninian founds a church at Whithorn
563	St Columba arrives on Iona
c. 500	Scots create the kingdom of Dalriada
597	Death of St Columba
638	Edinburgh falls to the Angles
685	Pictish victory over the Angles at Nechtansmere
794	First recorded Viking raid in Scotland
806	Vikings raid Iona, killing 68 monks
c. 843	Kenneth MacAlpin unites the Picts and the Scots
c. 880	Earldom of Orkney founded
1018	Malcolm II defeats the Angles at Carham
1040	Macbeth ascends the throne
1124	David I crowned king
1165	Accession of William the Lion
1174	Treaty of Falaise forces William the Lion to do homage to Henry II for Scotland
1263	Norsemen defeated at the battle of Largs
1297	Wallace defeats the English at Stirling Bridge
1305	Execution of Wallace
1306	Coronation of Robert the Bruce
1314	Bruce wins victory at Bannockburn
1320	Declaration of Arbroath
1388	Scots defeat the English at the battle of Otterburn
1513	Scottish forces defeated at Flodden
1542	Accession of Mary Queen of Scots
1547	Battle of Pinkie results in defeat of the Scots
1572	Death of John Knox
1587	Execution of Mary Queen of Scots
1603	James VI ascends throne of England
1692	Massacre at Glencoe
1707	Act of Union between England and Scotland
1715	First Jacobite rebellion
1745	Bonnie Prince Charlie launches second Jacobite uprising
1746	Scottish defeat at the battle of Culloden

GLOSSARY

Blockhouse	Block-shaped stone fort.
Broch	A circular drystone tower, used as a fortified dwelling in the pre-Christian period; brochs are mainly found in the far north.
Cairn	Mound of stones, usually covering a burial chamber.
Cist	A single grave, made of stone slabs.
Court cairn	Chamber tomb with a crescent-shaped 'court' at its entrance.
Crannog	Fortified dwelling, constructed on an artificial island.
Cross-slab	Rectangular slab bearing a cross, carved in high relief; distinct from a Celtic cross, where the stone itself has been sculpted into the shape of a cross.
Cup-mark	Cup-shaped hollow, carved into a stone; often encircled by a carved ring, hence the term cup-and-ring mark.
Dalriada	First colony founded in Scotland by the ancient Scots; there was also a Dalriada in Ireland.
Henge	Stone circle with surrounding earthworks; henges carried ritual overtones and often contained burial sites.
Jacobite	Supporter of James VII (James II of England) and his descendants.
Midden	Refuse heap in a prehistoric settlement, often containing food remains or fragments of artefacts.
Peel tower	Fortified tower-house, usually entered on the first floor via a ladder; particularly common in the Borders.
Quern	A stone for grinding cereal or seeds; often concave and sometimes used in conjunction with a rubbing stone.
Runes	Angular script, carved onto stone or wood; widely used by the Vikings.
Vitrified fort	Prehistoric stone fort with walls that have turned to a glassy mass, after subjection to intense heat; most common in Pictish territory.
Wheelhouse	Iron Age house with partition walls that project inwards, like the spokes of a wheel.

INDEX